All

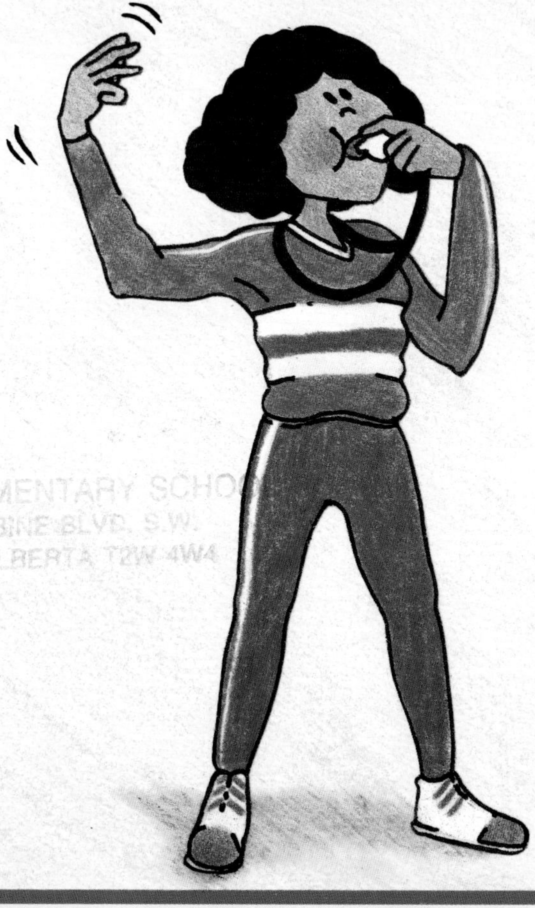

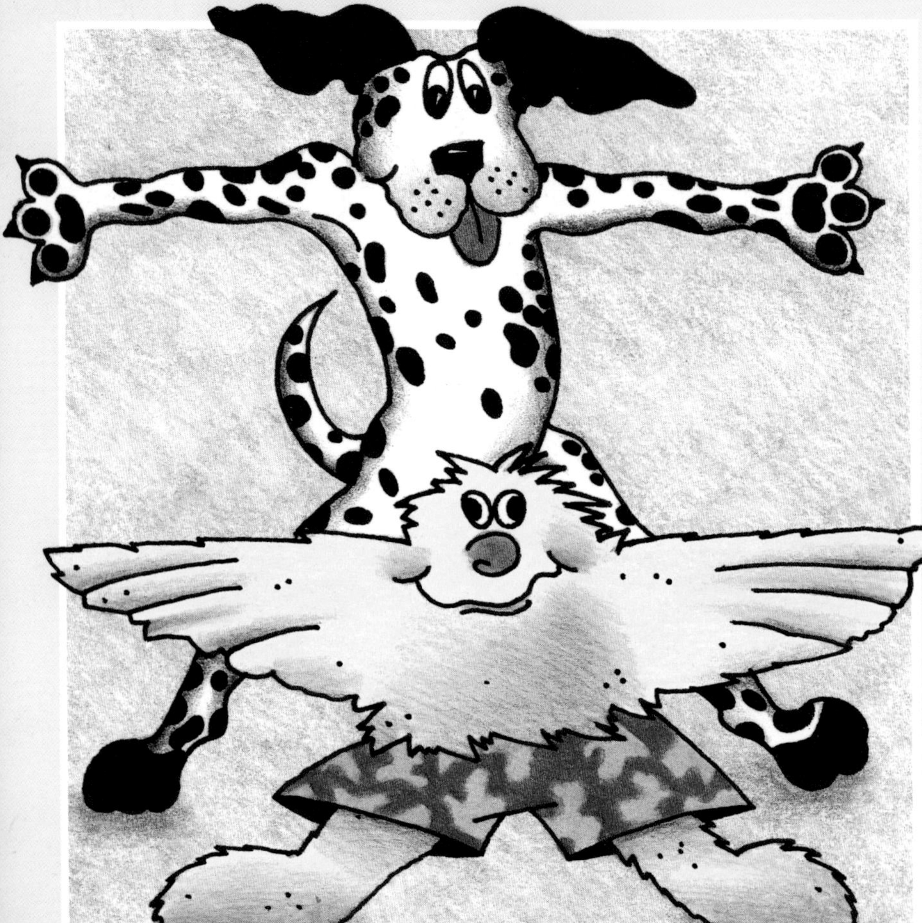

As wide as a gate,

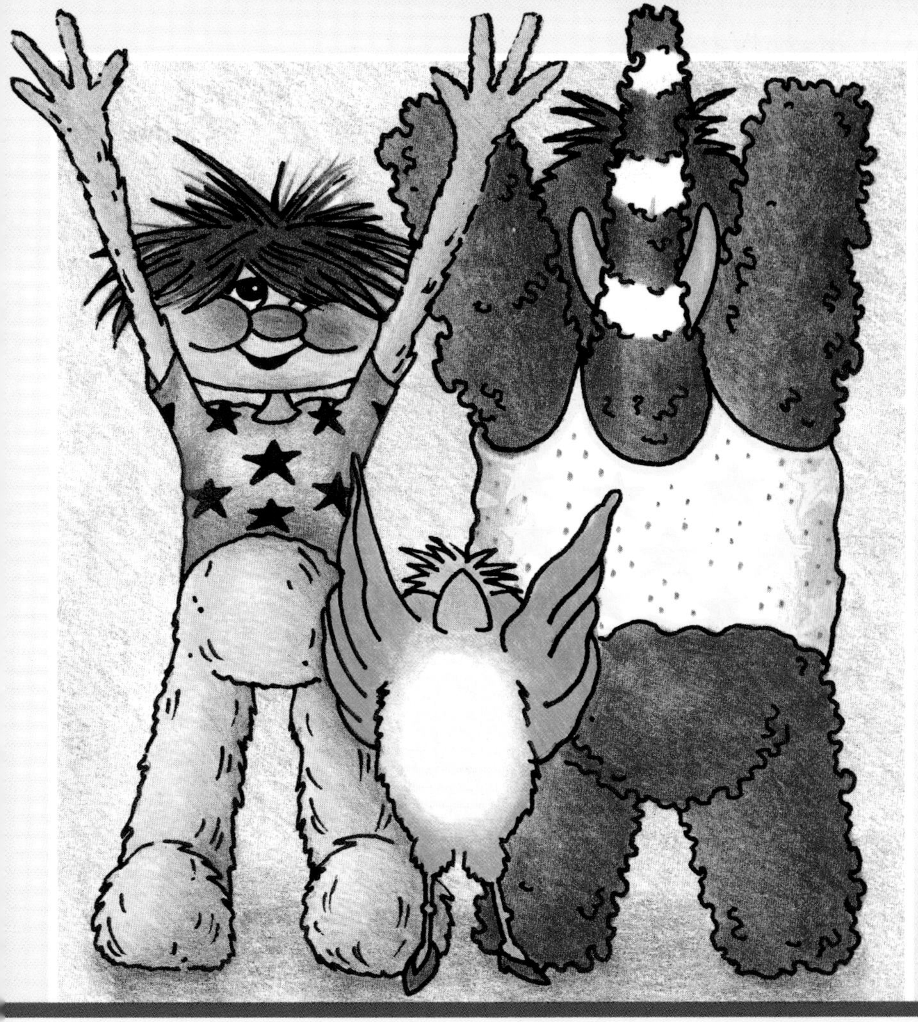

as tall as a house,

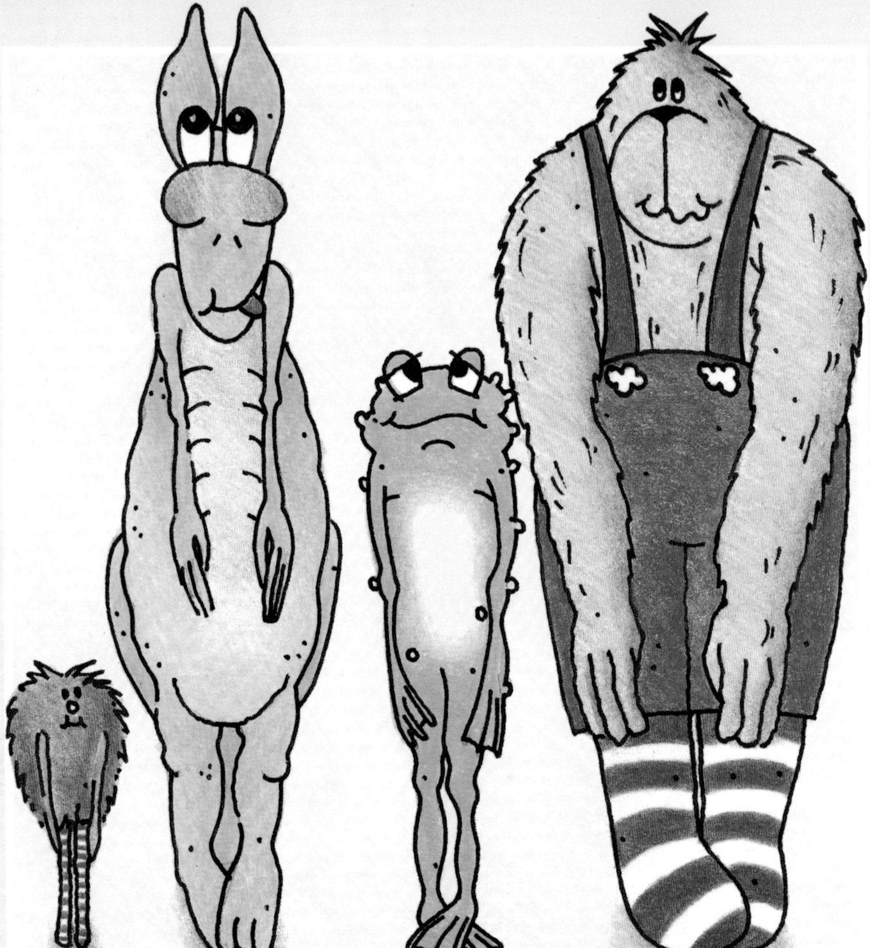

as thin as a pin,

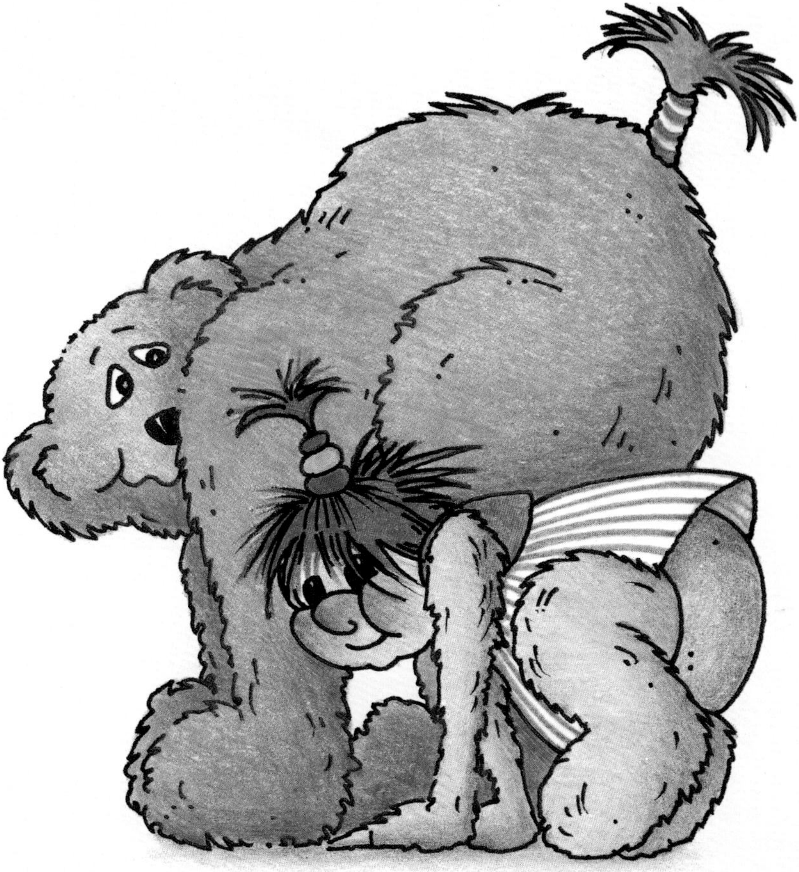

as small as a mouse,

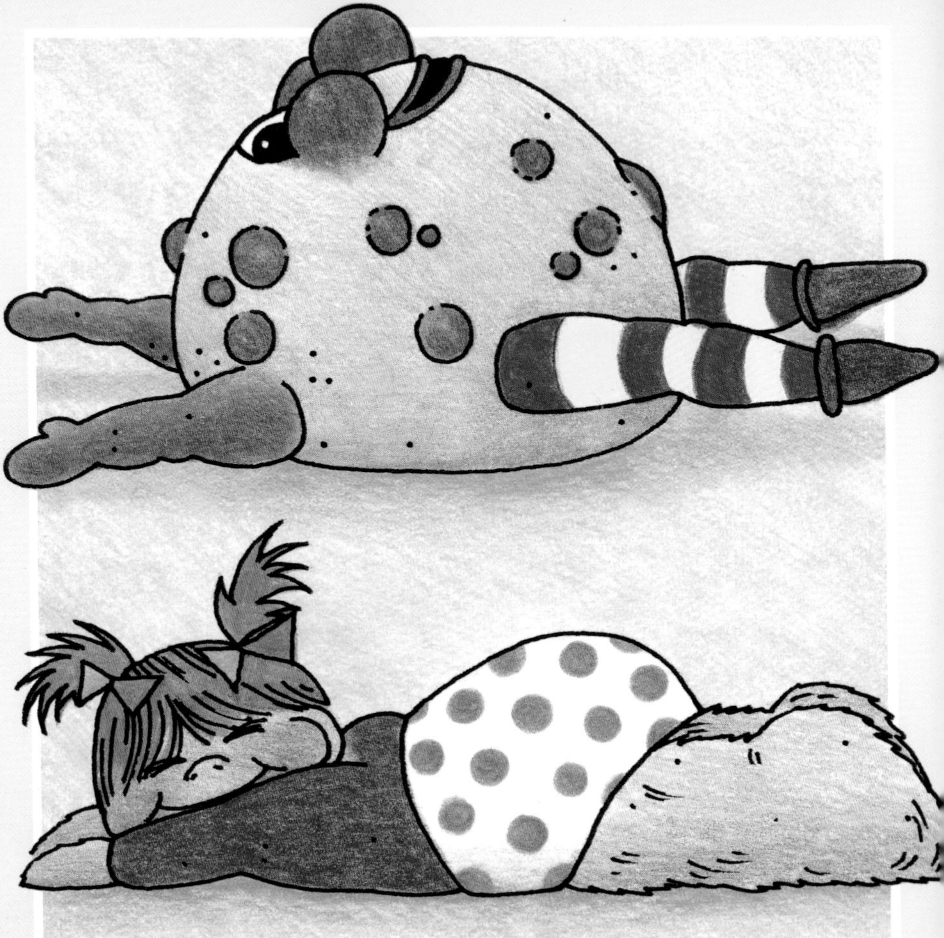

as long as a log,